# DOVER TO RAMSGATE

## including the Margate Sands branch

**Vic Mitchell and Keith Smith**

*First published June 1990*

*ISBN 0 906520 78 9*

© *Middleton Press 1990*

*Design and Laser typesetting -*
            *Deborah Goodridge*

*Published by Middleton Press*
            *Easebourne Lane*
            *Midhurst, West Sussex*
            *GU29 9AZ*
            *Tel. (0730) 813169*

*Printed & bound by Biddles Ltd,*
            *Guildford and Kings Lynn*

# CONTENTS

# ACKNOWLEDGEMENTS

In addition to those mentioned in the captions we would like to express our gratitude for the assistance from R.M.Casserley, P.Clarke, G.Croughton, J.Davis, Miss F.Edgar, A.French, P.Horn, N.Langridge, J.Miller, A.Mott, R.Randell, R.D.Smith, E.Staff, N.Stanyon and our meticulous wives.

The map shows the pre-1899 ownership of the main lines, together with the later minor railways. The inset map indicates the 1926 rearrangement of the Thanet lines and shows the new SR connection through Dumpton Park. (Railway Magazine)

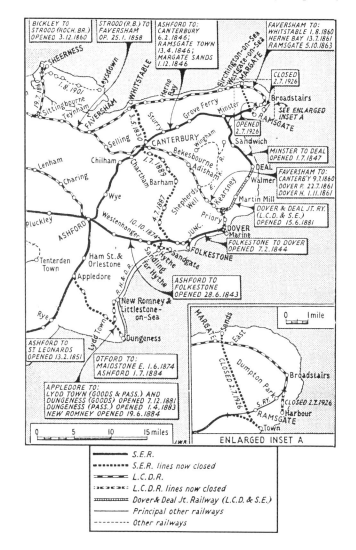

ENLARGED INSET A

S.E.R.
S.E.R. lines now closed
L.C.D.R.
L.C.D.R. lines now closed
Dover & Deal Jt. Railway (L.C.D. & S.E.)
Principal other railways
Other railways

# GEOGRAPHICAL SETTING

Dover is situated in the deep valley of the short River Dour, thus presenting travellers arriving at the port with a formidable climb by any route from the town, except along the coast line. The railway to Deal rises along the western side of the valley, crosses it and returns on the opposite side, in order to gain height to penetrate the upper chalk of the eastern end of the North Downs, by means of the 1412 yd. long Guston Tunnel.

The route runs off the dip slope of the chalk downs onto the level coastal alluvium between Walmer and Deal. At Sandwich, the line crosses an outcrop of Thanet Beds and then runs close to the greatly meandering River Stour.

After traversing Minster Marshes, the railway turns east and reaches the chalk mass of the Isle of Thanet at Cliffs End, the towns of

Ramsgate and Margate being old established settlements on this stable deposit.

All maps in this book are to the scale of 25" to 1 mile, unless otherwise indicated.

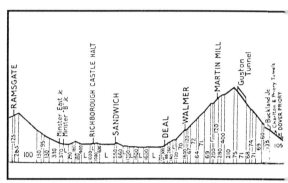

# HISTORICAL BACKGROUND

The South Eastern Railway opened the line from Ashford to Ramsgate (Town) and Margate (Sands) in 1846, its Ashford to Dover route having been completed in 1844.

A branch from Minster to Deal came into use on 1st July 1847 and was operated by the SER. Its competitor in the area, the London, Chatham & Dover Railway, opened to Dover on 22nd July 1861. It effectively prevented the SER linking its stations at Dover and Deal. After a prolonged period of acrimony between the two companies, a joint line between these two places was proposed during a period of relative harmony. The connection came into traffic on 15th June 1881 and was subsequently a cause of considerable friction between the rivals. Reason prevailed in 1899, when operations were put in the charge of a managing committee and the South Eastern &

Chatham Railway came into being.

The formation of the Southern Railway in 1923 resulted in the rationalisation of lines in the Thanet area. A connection was laid between the former competing lines and new stations built at Dumpton Park and Ramsgate. On 2nd July 1926, the new line was opened and those to Margate Sands and Ramsgate Harbour were closed.

The transition to British Railways in 1948 made little difference to the railways of the area. The long awaited electrification came to fruition on 2nd January 1961 but only a partial service was operated until June 1962.

The designation "down" is used throughout this album to refer to trains running from Dover to Ramsgate, although between Deal and Minster they were termed "up" until 1929.

# PASSENGER SERVICES

The modest service on the SER's branch to Deal had increased to eight weekday and four Sunday trains by 1869. The LCDR initially provided six trains between Kearsney and Deal, weekdays only. On weekdays in the 1880s several SER trains from Minster ran through to Dover Town and the LCDR provided a few journeys between Deal and Dover Priory. Each company worked the entire route on alternate Sundays.

The table below gives an indication of the intensity of services to Deal, in war and peace.

|      | From the north - | | From the south - | |
|------|----------|---------|----------|---------|
|      | Weekdays | Sundays | Weekdays | Sundays |
| 1890 | 15 | 6  | 5  | 2  |
| 1906 | 15 | 10 | 25 | 13 |
| 1917 | 8  | 5  | 15 | 7  |
| 1928 | 25 | 17 | 29 | 17 |
| 1944 | 10 | 6  | 15 | 4  |
| 1958 | 23 | 15 | 18 | 13 |

From 1881 until 1926, most of the trains from the north originated at Margate Sands and reversed at Ramsgate Town. Most of those from the south ran from Dover, although a few were routed via or originated at Kearsney.

The timetable remained unchanged with the introduction of electric services in January 1961, as many trains continued to be steam hauled. It was not until 18th June 1962, that a regular-interval all-electric service was introduced, bringing to an end the termination of trains at Deal. The basic timetable gave two trains an hour on the route, one reversing at Minster. The frequency was reduced to hourly in May 1982, the Minster reversals having been limited to a few peak hour trains, Mondays to Fridays, since May 1981.

Since electrification, trains have originated at Margate or Ramsgate and travelled to London (Charing Cross) via Folkestone, with one or two business services to Cannon Street.

DEAL, SANDWICH, MINSTER JUNCTION, RAMSGATE, and MARGATE.—South Eastern.

DOVER, DEAL, RAMSGATE TOWN, and MARGATE SANDS.—South Eastern and Chatham.

a Do not stop at Ebbsfleet and Cliffsend Halt.   * Station is adjacent to Ewell and River.
† Station for Kingsdown.   ¶ "Halt" at Ebbsfleet and Cliffsend, between Minster Junction and St. Lawrence.

# DOVER PRIORY

1. From left to right in this southward view of 1876 we see the goods shed, the roof over the passenger station, a double-armed signal post and the four-road carriage shed. This obscures the locomotive shed, only its ventilators being visible. The most distant of the five locomotives is standing on the turntable. (Lens of Sutton)

The functions of the various buildings shown on this 1866 survey are described in caption no.1.

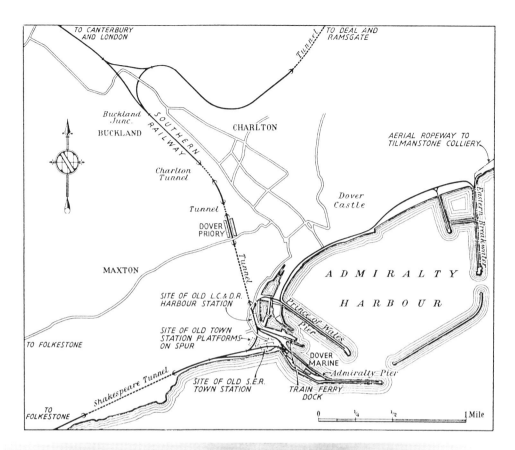

2. A northward view through the arches of Folkestone Road bridge has the carriage shed and goods loop on the left and the two platforms with the overall roof in the centre. This signal box seen at the end of the up platform was in use until 1930, "up" being to Victoria LCDR. (Lens of Sutton)

← ───────

The SER 1844 station was close to the waterfront and is described and illustrated in our *Ashford to Dover* album, along with the later Dover Marine station, now Western Docks. The LCDR's first terminus opened on 22nd July 1861 and was known as Dover Town until being renamed Priory in July 1863. It ceased to be a terminus on 1st November 1861 after which trains ran through Dover Tunnel to the Harbour station. (Railway Magazine)

3. Hotels flank the goods yard gates which are close to the telephone pole. For many years a siding from the yard passed through a gate to the Ordnance Depot. (Lens of Sutton)

4. In 1906, the SER purchased eight steam railcars from Kitson & Co. No. 5, illustrated here, and no. 7 were allocated to Dover and worked a frequent service to Sandgate, reversing at Sandling Junction.
(Lens of Sutton)

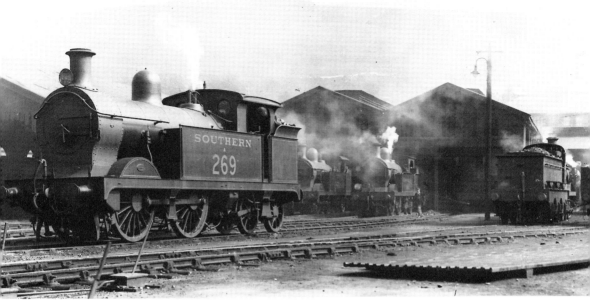

5. Lack of wind caused the smoke to linger on 14th May 1927 as H class no. A269 waited ready for duty. The locomotives were transferred to a new depot on the seafront in 1928, a move no doubt regretted during stormy weather. (H.C.Casserley)

6. The overall roof and the goods shed are evident as the driver looks back from no. A315, one of Mr. Wainwright's elegant E class 4-4-0s. Until 1931, the SR used the prefix A (for Ashford) on former SECR engines. (H.C.Casserley)

7. A major reconstruction of the station took place in 1932, following the demolition of the carriage shed, locomotive depot and overall roof. This picture was taken from the new up island platform and includes the old goods shed (left) and part of the roof of the new one on the extreme right. (P.Rutherford)

8. In 1932, the down platform received a new canopy with rivetted steel facing of standard SR design. Ex-LSWR class T9 no. 726 runs in with the 11.18am Ramsgate to Charing Cross service on 29th April 1938. It ran via Dover Marine, reversing there. (D.H.Wakely / J.R.W.Kirkby)

9. Dover was under heavy enemy bombardment for much of WWII and nearly half the residents moved away, most of those remaining sleeping in caves in the hills. The station was damaged many times, but most severely on 13th September 1944 when there were several fatalities. Trains were often delayed by passengers sheltering in the tunnels. (H.C.Casserley)

10. This and the previous picture were taken in April 1947 when the stanchions still bore white painted bands to aid their detection in the blackout. Class L1 no. 1787 is at the head of a Ramsgate to Charing Cross train. (H.C.Casserley)

11. A 1953 photograph features the luggage lift shaft, one of many modern details incorporated in the rebuilt station. Only the railings survived the rebuilding. Below the SR sign is the BR London fare - 11s9d. (D.Cullum)

12. The early morning sun throws long shadows on class D1 4-4-0 no. 31739 as it arrives with the 7.24 am from London Bridge on 20th September 1958. In the up loop, which was signalled for reversible running, is class Q1 no. 33040 with the 10.15 am departure for the Chatham line. (J.H.Aston)

13. The 10-ton crane is visible between the goods shed and the lofty water tank, in this September 1968 panorama. Goods services were withdrawn on 3rd July 1961 but most of

the sidings were retained for storage of coaches and vans. The white segment (top left) is the first cutting on the Deal line, seen on the cover of this book. (J.Scrace)

14. The platform lines are on the gradient of 1 in 104, evident by the level siding on the left of this 1987 view. In 1990, three short sidings and one long electrified one were still retained. All three platforms have been signalled for reversible running, since the introduction of colour lights on 27th April 1980. (J.Scrace)

15. No. 47422 emerges from Priory Tunnel on 4th July 1989, with the 06.18 Manchester Piccadily to Folkestone Central service. The up loop points are seen near the tunnel mouth, the brick wall making platform 3 shorter than the others. The signal box came into use on 16th November 1930. (J.Scrace)

16. In 1989, the exterior had a distinctive appearance, devoid of a BR logo. In addition to the daily Manchester service, the station was served by four trains an hour to London; two to Charing Cross and two to Victoria. (J.Scrace)

North of Dover, the line passes through Priory Tunnel (158 yds) and Charlton Tunnel (264 yds) before reaching the triangular junction with the Deal line. The 1906 survey at 6" to 1 mile reveals the severity of the curve required to cross the Dour Valley.

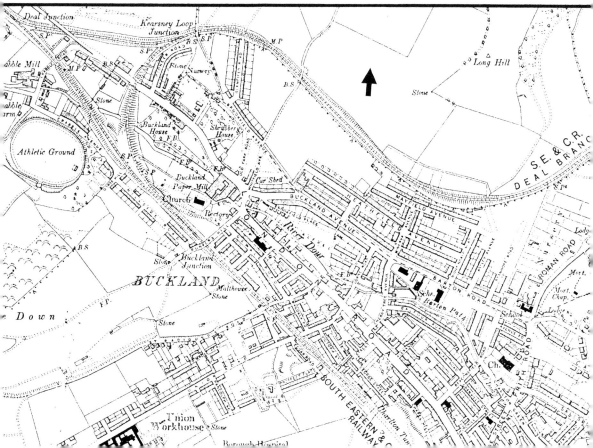

# NORTH OF DOVER

17. Buckland Junction is one mile north of Dover Priory and is where the Deal line diverges to the right from the former LCDR main line to Faversham. The signal box closed on 7th December 1980, since when the junction has been controlled from Dover Priory. South of the junction, a siding on the west side of the line served Dover Gasworks. (D.Cullum)

18. One of the powerful Schools class, no. 30938 *St. Olave's* climbs the curve between Buckland Junction and Kearsney Loop Junction on 15th March 1953, with the 9.36am Charing Cross to Ramsgate. A 30 mph speed limit applies on the curve. (D.Cullum)

19. The lines on the left connect with Kearsney and had never carried a frequent service, but were much used by military traffic during the wars and were of value again during the early part of 1953, when trains were diverted away from the North Kent coast due to the effects of the severe flooding. No. 30803 King Arthur class *Sir Harry le Fise Lake* proceeds towards Dover on 11th May 1952. (J.J.Smith)

20. The loop was not required for the electric timetable but the elevated box remained in use until 7th December 1980. The loop was opened on 1st July 1882 by the LCDR, thus enabling them to compete with the SER for the London - Deal traffic. The SER retaliated by threatening to exclude LCDR trains from *their* station at Deal ! (J.Scrace)

# TILMANSTONE AERIAL ROPEWAY

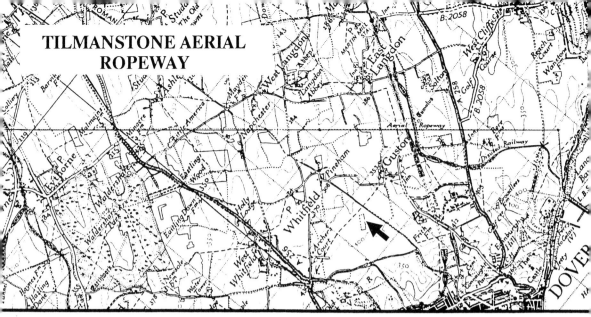

The horizontal line across this 1" survey of 1936 indicates the route of the ropeway. Also marked is the then disused contractor's line from Martin Mill to the cliff top above Dover Harbour, described in detail later. The ropeway crossed the railway north of the 1412 yd. long Guston Tunnel and provided the SR with serious competition. Prior to WWI rail freight charges to Dover were 5/9 per ton, more than half the cost of mining the coal ! Transport by ropeway was *one tenth* of the cost.

21. One of the two "bridges" over public roads is seen near Tilmanstone Colliery in 1950. Started in 1906, the mine became productive in 1913 but was bankrupt by 1925. An enterprising new owner saw the need for an independent transport system to Dover Harbour and the first part of the ropeway was officially opened on 12th October 1929. (Col. Stephens Railway Archives)

22. Half way along the main route, near Napchester, a transfer station was built. Here the buckets were transferred, via steel rails, to the next length of rope. It was described as a "Divide station", as three other ropeways were to be erected from this point. They were to convey coal to proposed industries - a massive cement works north of Dover, a carbonisation plant producing chemicals, coke and gas for the towns of East Kent and finally blast furnaces and a steel works. The event is the opening day in 1929.
(Col. Stephens Railway Archives)

23. To reach the harbour, the ropes passed through two parallel tunnels, shown as black dots on the cliff face, to the right of the crane. These were not ready until 14th February 1930, when the system started to carry 120 tons per hour, each bucket holding 14.5 cwt. - about 0.75 tonne. Two eight hour shifts were sometimes worked, but reliability was poor. (Col. Stephens Railway Archives)

24. On the Eastern Arm a bunker of 5000 ton capacity was built, which was able to discharge up to 750 tons per hour. The system was little used after 1935, became redundant with the advent of WWII and was dismantled in 1954. (Col. Stephens Railway Archives)

# MARTIN MILL

25. A mixed bag of coaches arrive from the north during the SECR era. This was designated an up train although it would use the down line south of Buckland Junction and through Dover Priory. (Lens of Sutton)

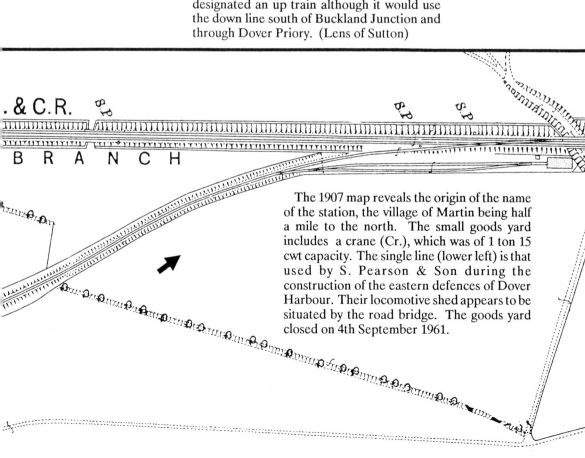

The 1907 map reveals the origin of the name of the station, the village of Martin being half a mile to the north. The small goods yard includes a crane (Cr.), which was of 1 ton 15 cwt capacity. The single line (lower left) is that used by S. Pearson & Son during the construction of the eastern defences of Dover Harbour. Their locomotive shed appears to be situated by the road bridge. The goods yard closed on 4th September 1961.

26. Another northward view shows the good weather protection provided in this windswept area. The down side now only has a small glazed shelter but the up canopy has been reclad, the original stanchions being retained. (Lens of Sutton)

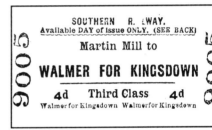

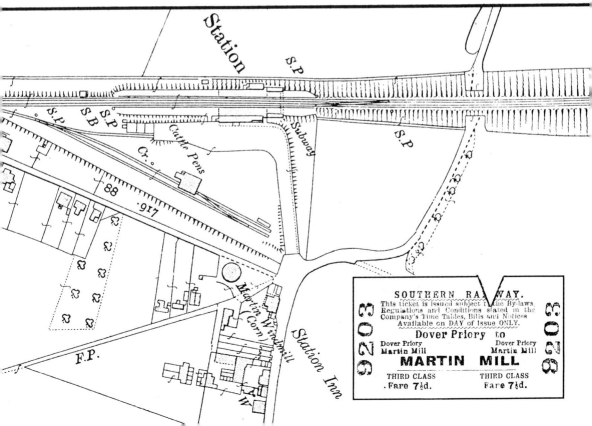

27. The signal box shown on the map (SB) was closed on 7th October 1934 and a frame was installed in the booking office, thus reducing manpower. The tallest instrument in this 1958 photograph is a Walker's block and probably dated from the opening of the line. Three levers were still in use in 1990, with three-way instruments to Deal and track circuiting southwards. (P.Hay)

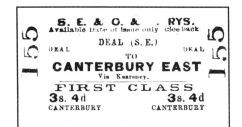

29. As at Amberley, the booking clerk/ signalman also acted as a sub - postmaster for many years. The small canopy and the seat have been lost since this photograph was taken in 1961. (Prof.H.P.White)

28. No. 34005 *Barnstaple* draws level with the cattle dock buffer stops on 6th September 1958. In the distance is the upper quadrant up home signal and part of the curved roof over the subway steps. (P.Hay)

30. Traffic has never been heavy, as witnessed on 4th September 1968. Most potential passengers live about two miles south-east of the station, at St. Margaret's at Cliffe and at St. Margaret's Bay, the starting point for many cross - channel swimmers. (J.Scrace)

31. Amazingly, the gates and railings to the station approach were still standing in 1990, having survived WWII when most were melted down and transformed into armaments. (V.Mitchell)

Martin Mill (top right) was the starting point for a single line laid down in 1897 to facilitate the transport of materials for the construction of the Eastern Arm of the Admiralty's Harbour. Terminating 300ft. above the work site, a balanced rope-worked incline was used as the means of lowering ballast to the foreshore. The work was finished in 1909 when approval was obtained to convert the line to a 3ft 6in gauge electric tramway but the scheme never materialised, the original track being lifted in 1937. (Railway Magazine)

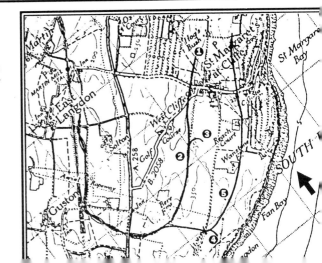

The 1936 survey at 1" to 1 mile has the approximate positions of the military railway and installations added to it.

1. *Pooh*
2. *Winnie*
3. Gun Spurs
4. Gun Spur
5. Line serving batteries of other guns

32. In order to erect and serve two massive clifftop guns, most of the contractor's line was relaid during WWII and re-opened on 26th July 1940. The first gun (named *Winnie* after Prime Minister Churchill who authorised it) had a 14" barrel weighing 97 tons. It was first fired across the channel on 22nd August 1940 and had to be replaced in December after 47 firings. The second gun *(Pooh)* was ready on 9th February 1941 and used shells weighing 1590lbs. These static guns were vulnerable to attack and so three 13.5" rail mounted guns were obtained -

*Scene Shifter* - September 1940
*Piecemaker* - November 1940
*Gladiator* - May 1941

An even larger 18" gun arrived in November 1941 and was named *Boche Buster*. Four LMS 0-6-0 diesels were allocated to them, together with a train composed of vechicles for ammunition, sleeping, cooking, stores etc. They could only be fired in line with the track and so a fan of three curved spurs was laid out on the cliff top. The guns were stored in nearby tunnels, such as Guston, through which passenger trains then ran on the remaining line which was operated as a single line. A series of rotatable rail mounted weapons with 9.2" and 12" barrels were also developed, these being operable from almost any siding. A view from above West Cliffe shows the curved tracks, the cliff of South Foreland being in the background. (R.Hollingsby coll.)

33. St. Margaret's is the probable location of this rare picture of *Piecemaker*. The van was for ammunition and was of French origin, having been stranded in Britain at the outbreak of war. (Royal Marines Museum)

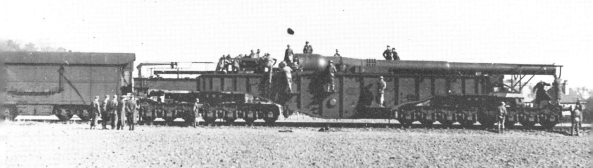

# WALMER

34. A northward view from the up platform includes the signal box and part of the goods yard. Our ancestors paid attention to detail, such as finials on railway posts.
(Lens of Sutton)

35. On 6th August 1958, BR class 4 2-6-4T no. 80011 brings in the through train from Birkenhead, which ran via Reading, Redhill and Dover. Although slow, the train was well patronised in the summer. (P.Hay)

36. With the timbers encrusted with oil and ash of numerous locomotives standing at the end of the down platform, the conductor rails wait to serve the new trains. The presence of the crossover meant that one live rail had to be undesirably close to the up platform and so was provided with protection boards. (D.Collyer coll.)

The 1906 edition marks the position of the 10-ton crane, the adjacent siding accommodating a rail mounted gun during WWII. During that time, several American servicemen were killed when petrol exploded while it was being loaded near the goods shed.

38. A photograph from July 1989 shows the subway approach on each platform and the line dropping away northwards at 1 in 70, a 45 mph speed limit applying to down trains on this length. (J.Scrace)

The yard closed on 2nd October 1961 and the signal box followed on 29th November 1964. There is now only one road to the station - the shorter one, although a footpath is retained to the north.

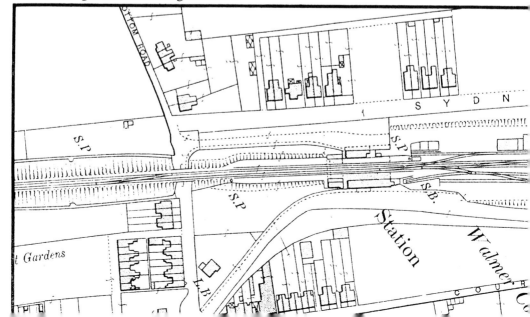

37. Although similar to Martin Mill, the main building is nearly twice as long and included a covered goods entrance to the platforms. Major renovation work took place in the summer of 1989, the results being seen in February 1990. (V.Mitchell)

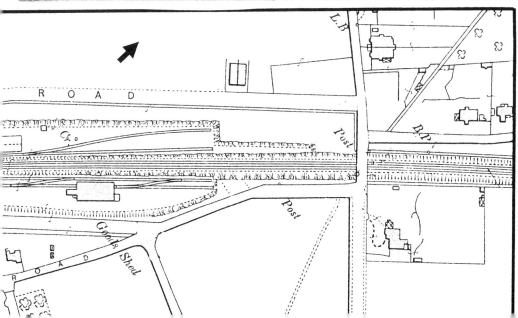

# DEAL

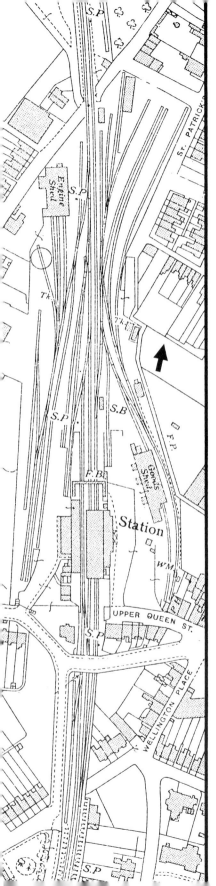

39. The station was a terminus from 1847 to 1881, trains using the two lines on the left. One of the 118 class 2-4-0s waits to depart for Minster Junction from the new platform in about 1895. (D.Cullum coll.)

The 1938 map marks the position of the engine shed, which ceased to be used as such in 1930. It had replaced a smaller two-road structure in about 1880.

40. In the steam era, many trains terminated here, involving much shunting and much labour. No. 249 is one of the class 01 0-6-0s used mainly for freight work. In the mid-1930s the town had a population of about 22,000. Improvements carried out in 1873 involved the elimination of the ticket platform north of the station and the provision of a new signal box and a refreshment room. (Lens of Sutton)

41. The building on the west side of the line was opened in 1881 and was of the same style as the stations to the south. Note the contemporary way of moving house - a pantechnicon on a flat wagon.
(Lens of Sutton)

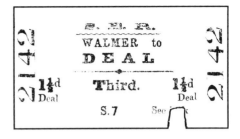

42. Seen in 1921, the original SER appears to be deriving the maximum revenue from advertising, while the roof has lost its sheeting above the centre track. (P.Rutherford)

43. Further decay of the roof is evident as temporary supports have been added near two of the stanchions. Note the position of the signal box and the double sided water column. (Lens of Sutton)

44. No. 45388 heads an excursion from Bletchley on 29th July 1956, the first day of through working engines from the London Midland Region to Deal. It is passing the short siding south of the roadbridge. (S.C.Nash)

45. A 1957 view from the footbridge shows that a canopy replaced the old roof over the up platform and that the 1881 building retained its ornate valance. The up starting signal, just visible beyond the road bridge, projects over a neighbour's garden and was still in use in 1990. (D.Clayton)

46. Turning round, we see the revised position of the signal box, the 8-ton crane, the water tank and the former engine shed (left of centre). Its brick gable end had been replaced by asbestos sheeting. (D.Clayton)

47. The Railway Enthusiats Club's railtour on 23rd May 1959 is also seen in pictures 14 and 26 in our *East Kent Light Railway,* the van being for participants' bicycles. This siding still remained in place in 1990, the sole survivor of the goods yard which closed on 1st May 1972. (J.H.Aston)

48. On the same day, class N no. 31853 waits with the 3.2pm service from Ramsgate to Cannon Street. Conductor rails lie in the "four-foot", awaiting their insulators. (J.H.Aston)

49. The up side, seen in 1962, is of notably different design to the other buildings on the route and remained largely intact in 1990, apart from the loss of the awning. The down side structures were demolished earlier. (Prof.H.P.White)

50. The new signal box came into use on the 14th May 1939. The gates were replaced by barriers, operated from the box, on 21st October 1973. The next crossing north is North Wall, this receiving light signals in June 1972. (J.Scrace)

51. Passengers emerge from the two economical glass shelters on the down platform as a Ramsgate bound train arrives on 22nd June 1989. Little evidence remains of the once busy goods yards, although coal is still stored on the up side. (S.C.Nash)

## THROUGH EXPRESS TRAIN SERVICE BETWEEN
### SANDWICH, DEAL, DOVER, FOLKESTONE, MARGATE, RAMSGATE, HASTINGS, EASTBOURNE, BRIGHTON,
AND
### BIRMINGHAM, WOLVERHAMPTON, SHREWSBURY, CHESTER, BIRKENHEAD
**WEEK DAYS ONLY.**

**From SOUTH to NORTH.**

| Station | SATURDAYS ONLY. Until 28th August. Through Train—Margate to Birmingham. | SATURDAYS ONLY. Through Carriages—Hastings, Eastbourne and Brighton to Wolverhampton. | SATURDAYS ONLY. Through Train—Margate to Wolverhampton. | Refreshment Car and Through Carriages—Margate to Birkenhead, also on Mondays to Fridays from Hastings, Eastbourne and Brighton. Through Carriages—Folkestone to Birkenhead, Sandwich, Deal, Dover and Brighton. | SATURDAYS ONLY. Through Carriages—Hastings, Eastbourne and Brighton to Birmingham. |
|---|---|---|---|---|---|
| | a.m. | a.m. | a.m. | a.m. | p.m. |
| Sandwich ... dep. | … | … | … | 9 A11 | … |
| Deal ... ,, | … | … | … | 9 A21 | … |
| Walmer ... ,, | … | … | … | 9 A26 | … |
| Martin Mill ... ,, | … | … | … | 9 A33 | … |
| Dover Priory ... ,, | … | … | … | 9 A46 | … |
| Folkestone Central ¶¶ ... ,, | … | … | … | 10A 6 | … |
| Shorncliffe ... ,, | … | … | … | 10 11 | … |
| Margate ... dep. | 8 A55 | … | 9 A10 | 9C18 | … |
| Broadstairs ... ,, | … | … | 9 A19 | 9C26 | … |
| Dumpton Park ¶ ... ,, | … | … | … | 9 30 | … |
| Ramsgate ... ,, | … | … | 9 A27 | 9C35 | … |
| Minster (Thanet) ... ,, | … | … | 9 53 | 9 44 | … |
| Canterbury West ... ,, | … | … | … | 10 3 | … |
| Ashford (Kent) ... dep. | … | … | 10 18 | 10 34 | … |
| Tonbridge ... ,, | … | … | … | 11 9 | … |
| Hastings ... dep. | … | 8A48 | … | 9SXC25 | 12A18 |
| St. Leonards (Warrior Square) ... ,, | … | 8A52 | … | 9SXC27 | 12A22 |
| St. Leonards (West Marina) ... ,, | … | 8 56 | … | … | 12 26 |
| Bexhill Central ... ,, | … | 9 A4 | … | 9SXC36 | 12A35 |
| Eastbourne ... ,, | … | 9A11 | … | 10SXC3 | 12A40 |
| Seaford ... ,, | … | 9E10 | … | 9SXE36 | 12E44 |
| Brighton * ... ,, | … | 10 10 | … | 10SX45 | 1 35 |
| Redhill ... dep. | 10 47 | … | 11 28 | 11 40 | 2 18 |
| | | | p.m. | p.m. | |
| Guildford ... ,, | … | … | 12 5 | 12 16 | 2 56 |
| North Camp ... ,, | … | … | … | 12 31 | … |
| Reading General ... arr. | … | … | … | 12 58 | 3 45 |
| | p.m. | p.m. | | | |
| Reading General ... dep. | … | … | … | 1 6 | 3 52 |
| Oxford ... arr. | … | 2 0 | … | 1 43 | 4 35 |
| Banbury General ... ,, | 1 9 | … | 2 9 | 2 23 | 5 8 |
| Leamington Spa General ... ,, | 1 39 | … | 2 37 | 2 51 | 5 36 |
| Birmingham (Snow Hill) ... ,, | 2 15 | 2 37 | 3 14 | 3 23 | 6 15 |
| Wolverhampton (Low Level) ... ,, | 2B51 | 3 2 | 3 40 | 3 48 | 6B53 |
| Wellington ... ,, | 3B44 | 3D44 | … | 4 21 | 7B43 |
| Shrewsbury ... ,, | 4 B1 | 4D1 | … | 4 36 | 7B58 |
| Gobowen ... ,, | 4B31 | 4D31 | … | 5 4 | 8 B28 |
| Ruabon ... ,, | 4B44 | 4D44 | … | 5 18 | 8 B40 |
| Wrexham General ... ,, | 4B55 | 4D55 | … | 5 29 | 8 B50 |
| Chester General ... ,, | 5B22 | 5D22 | … | 6 1 | 9 B17 |
| Birkenhead Woodside ... ,, | 6 E0 | 6D0 | … | 6 37 | 9 B57 |

\* Frequent Electric trains between Bognor Regis, Littlehampton, Worthing and Brighton.
¶—For East Ramsgate.  ¶¶—For Sandgate.  A—Seats can be reserved 1/- per seat.
B—Change at Birmingham (Snow Hill).  C—Seats can be reserved 1/- per seat on Mondays to Fridays only.  D—Change at Wolverhampton (Low Level.)  E—Change at Brighton.  SX—Mondays to Fridays

Summer 1954

---

## LONDON & FOLKESTONE, DOVER, DEAL & SANDWICH.

### UP — MONDAYS TO FRIDAYS

| Station | a.m. | a.m. (R) | a.m. (R) | THE MAN OF KENT | a.m. (R) | a.m. | p.m. | p.m. | p.m. | p.m. (RF) |
|---|---|---|---|---|---|---|---|---|---|---|
| SANDWICH ...dep | 5 46 | 6 59 | 8A 8 | | 10A14 | 1145 | 1A 7 | 3A55 | 5 32 | 7 25 |
| Deal ... ,, | 5 54 | 7 10 | 8A16 | | 10A23 | 1155 | 1A16 | 4A 4 | 5 42 | 7 34 |
| Walmer ... ,, | 5 59 | 7 16 | 8A21 | | 10A28 | 12 0 | 1A21 | 4A 9 | 5 48 | 7 40 |
| Martin Mill ... ,, | … | 7 24 | 8A23 | | 10A35 | 12 8 | 1A29 | 4A16 | 5 56 | 7 48 |
| Dover Priory ... ,, | 6 19 | 7 38 | 8A41 | | 10A49 | 1221 | 1A42 | 4A34 | 6 12 | 8 1 |
| Folkestone C.B. ... ,, | 6 42 | 8 0 | 9A 0 | | 11A10 | 1245 | 2A 8 | 4A50 | 6 33 | 8 23 |
| LONDON | | | | | | | | | | |
| ,, Cannon Street arr | … | 9 30 | … | | … | … | … | … | … | … |
| ,, Charing Cross ,, | 8 42 | … | 10 38 | | 12 39 | 2 55 | 3 46 | 6 20 | 8 41 | 1049 |

### UP — SATURDAYS

| Station | a.m. | a.m. (R) | a.m. (R) | THE MAN OF KENT | a.m. | a.m. | a.m. (R) |
|---|---|---|---|---|---|---|---|
| SANDWICH ...dep | 5 46 | 6 59 | 8A 9 | | … | … | 10A 1 |
| Deal ... ,, | 5 54 | 7 10 | 8A17 | | 9A40 | 9A47 | 10A15 |
| Walmer ... ,, | 5 59 | 7 16 | 8A22 | | 9A47 | … | 10A21 |
| Martin Mill ... ,, | … | 7 24 | 8A30 | | 9A55 | … | 10A23 |
| Dover Priory ... ,, | 6 19 | 7 38 | 8A43 | | 10A10 | … | 10A36 |
| Folkestone C.B. ... ,, | 6 42 | 8 0 | 9A 3 | | 10A27 | … | 10A56 |
| LONDON | | | | | | | |
| ,, Cannon Street arr | … | 9 30 | … | | … | … | … |
| ,, Charing Cross ,, | 8c42 | … | 10 38 | | 12 20 | … | 12 26 |

### UP — SATURDAYS—continued

| Station | a.m. | p.m. | p.m. (R) | p.m. | p.m. | p.m. | p.m. |
|---|---|---|---|---|---|---|---|
| SANDWICH ...dep | 11k22 | … | 1 7 | 2 28 | 3A55 | 5 32 | 7 25 |
| Deal ... ,, | 11 20 | 12A20 | 1 16 | 2 40 | 4A 4 | 5 42 | 7 34 |
| Walmer ... ,, | 11 27 | 12A26 | 1 21 | 2 46 | 4A 9 | 5 48 | 7 40 |
| Martin Mill ... ,, | 11 35 | 12A35 | 1 29 | 2 54 | 4A16 | 5 56 | 7 48 |
| Dover Priory ... ,, | 11 43 | 12A48 | 1 42 | 3 9 | 4A34 | 6 12 | 8 1 |
| Folkestone C.B. ... ,, | 12 8 | 1A11 | 2 8 | 3 31 | 4A50 | 6 33 | 8 23 |
| LONDON | | | | | | | |
| ,, Charing Cross arr | 2 28 | 2 51 | 3 47 | 5 38 | 6 20 | 8 41 | 1049 |

### UP — SUNDAYS

| Station | a.m. | a.m. (R) | a.m. | a.m. | p.m. | p.m. | p.m. | p.m. |
|---|---|---|---|---|---|---|---|---|
| SANDWICH ...dep | … | 8k 9 | 10A14 | 11A39 | 3A19 | 4 54 | 6 23 | 7 56 |
| Deal ... ,, | … | 8A14 | 10A24 | 11A48 | 3A28 | 5 36 | 6 32 | 8 5 |
| Walmer ... ,, | … | 8A20 | 10A30 | 11A53 | 3A33 | 9 6 | 6 38 | 8 10 |
| Martin Mill ... ,, | … | 8A27 | 10A37 | 12A 0 | 3A40 | 5 17 | 6 45 | 8 18 |
| Dover Priory ... ,, | 6 55 | 8A40 | 10A50 | 12A16 | 3A54 | 5 30 | 6 58 | 8 32 |
| Folkestone C.B. ... ,, | 7 16 | 9A 3 | 11A14 | 12A36 | 4A18 | 5 50 | 7 14 | 8 56 |
| LONDON | | | | | | | | |
| ,, Charing Cross arr | 9 19 | 10 57 | 1 14 | 2 36 | 6 18 | 7 25 | 9 5 | 11 1 |

A—Seats may be reserved at a fee of 1/- per seat, upon personal or postal request to the Station Master. Early application is advisable.  B—Station for Sandgate.  c—Arrives 8 46 a.m. 10th July to 21st August.  g—Via Ashford and Minster Jct.  k—Via Minster Jct. and Ashford.
R—Refreshment Car facilities available.  RF—Refreshment Car facilities London and Folkestone.

# BETTESHANGER COLLIERY

52. Steel manufacturer Dorman Long & Co purchased mineral rights in the area and harbour contractors S. Pearson & Son joined them to form Pearson & Dorman Long Ltd. in the early 1920s. The objective was to establish a colliery, steel works and port. The first requirement was a railway to convey materials required for shaft sinking, the starting ceremony taking place on 19th May 1924. Both Kent and imported iron ore would be used but only the colliery materialised. This February 1935 photograph shows the end of the two-mile long branch.
(Kent County Library)

### Betteshanger locomotives in the 1950s

| | | | |
|---|---|---|---|
| St. Alphege | 0-6-0T | Hudswell Clarke | 1344/18 |
| St. Edmund | 0-6-0T | " " | 1345/18 |
| St. Augustine | 0-6-0ST | " " | 1495/23 |
| St. Martin | 0-6-0ST | Avonside | 2064/31 |
| No. 9 | 0-6-0ST | Hunslet | 3825/54 |
| No. 10 | 0-6-0ST | " | 3827/54 |

The first four were owned by Pearson & Dorman Long Ltd, prior to nationalisation in 1948. The last two were purchased by the NCB in 1954, no. 9 being illustrated in picture no. 41 in **Industrial Railways of the South-East.** **(Middleton Press)**

1937 edition

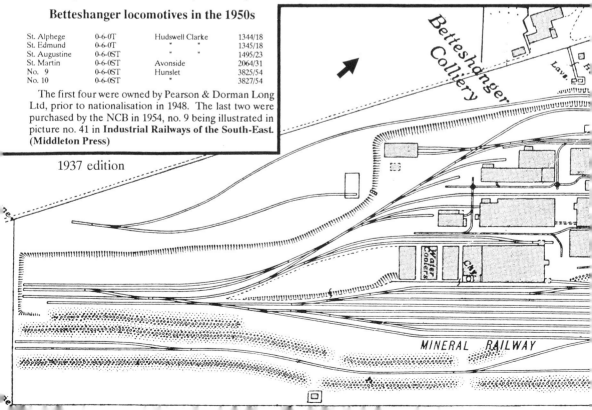

53. Until 10th January 1962, only a trailing connection to the down line was provided, controlled by a ground frame. At this time a facing crossover was added. In April 1976, the colliery railway system was abandoned and the branch reduced to under a mile in length. Twin 36" conveyor belts then moved the coal and waste from the colliery. Front loading shovels filled the trains from a concrete pad until the pit closure in August 1989, the last train running on the 12th. Output had dropped from over 12,000 tons per week to under 4,000. Waste minestone was transported from time to time, a notable example being for use during the reconstruction of the junctions between East Croydon and Selhurst. The box remained usable, but boarded up, in 1990. (B.M.Kidd)

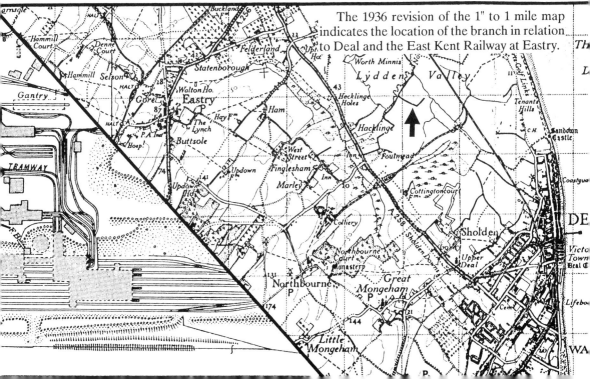

The 1936 revision of the 1" to 1 mile map indicates the location of the branch in relation to Deal and the East Kent Railway at Eastry.

# SANDWICH

54. Similar to the present building at Deal, Sandwich was more than doubled in size by extensions both east and west in 1892.

Curiously, this pre-extension view shows that one chimney stack lacks pots, a situation still prevailing in 1990. (J.Arnold coll.)

The 1898 map shows short sidings between the level crossing and the station, a similar arrangement being employed by the SER at Reigate.

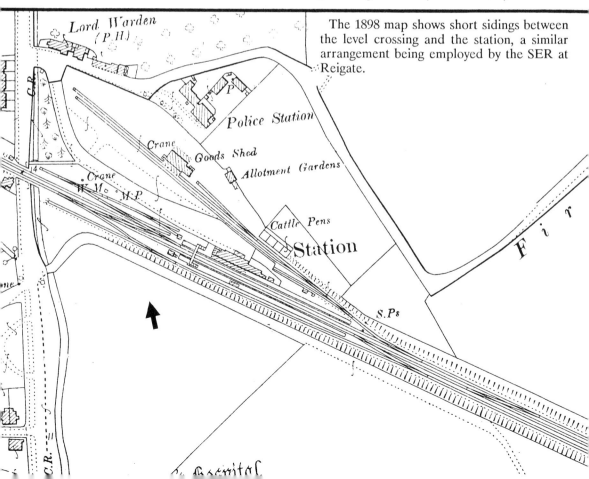

55. Compared with the previous photograph it is clear that a new approach road was constructed, presumably to allow for expansion of the goods yard. The 1892 signal box is at the end of the down platform - the site was abandoned on 30th January 1938, in favour of one close to the level crossing. (Lens of Sutton)

56. On the left, freight vehicles stand on the goods loop, which was a refuge siding with two trailing connections. An axle weight restriction on the bridge over North Stream (two miles south of Sandwich) prevented the heavy guns (and Schools class locomotives) reaching here during WWII. (D.Cullum coll.)

57. This June 1958 photograph is taken from the site of the earlier signal box. The goods loop on the right was retained for some time after the goods yard was closed on 7th October 1963. (H.C.Casserley)

58. A 1969 record of the signal box shows it when it still controlled semaphore signals and prior to the installation of barriers on 15th July 1973. In 1990 the block post was still operational. (J.Scrace)

59. A visit in 1989 reveals the historic station to be preserved in good order and even the down platform shelter to have survived. Its roof effectively deflects the south-west wind in this exposed location. (J.Scrace)

60. As at all other stations on the route, the booking office was still staffed, at least part time. Vandalism is thus reduced but unit no. 1606 had received signs from simple minded idiots and so the photograph has been touched up to eliminate them. (J.Scrace)

61. A southbound train passes over Ash Road, hauled by no. 171, a class O 0-6-0. This crossing received automatic half barriers on 27th January 1965, as did Richborough Crossing, half a mile to the north. Southwards, Woodnesborough Crossing was fitted with controlled barriers, with CCTV, on 18th December 1977. North-east of the crossing, a fourteen-wagon siding was opened in 1875, for the use by a local brewery. A second siding was added in 1889 and general traffic was handled. (Lens of Sutton)

62. A little over a mile north of Sandwich, the East Kent Light Railway passed over the SECR and then crossed the River Stour on an even more slender bridge (right). This branch from Eastry reached Richborough Port but was not passed for passenger traffic beyond Sandwich Road. (A.G.Wells)

63. A closer look at the EKR bridge over the main line confirms that it was constructed to the minimum specification. It was intended to carry a heavy traffic in coal for export from Richborough Port but in the event it carried very little. (Col. Stephens Railway Archives)

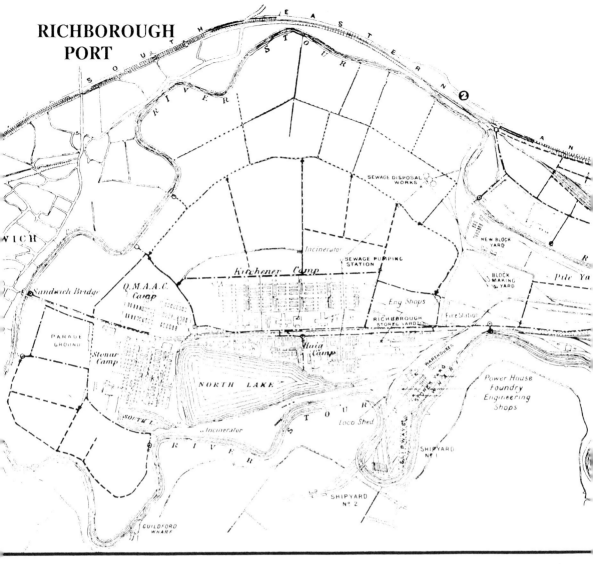

Work started in 1916 to create a port in the Stonar Estuary as Dover was a congested Naval harbour and could not handle the massive transport requirements of the Army. Over 2200 acres of marsh were drained and an amazing 60 miles of sidings were laid, some leading to the train ferry berth (lower right, 1). A halt for military personnel was built on the main line, near the N of SOUTH EASTERN (2). From 1919 until 1921, a train service was operated for the benefit of civilian workers from Dover and from Margate Sands. It ran to Saltpans (3), between the Robertson and Cowan Camps. Trains used the connections at both the north and south ends of the camp, although those arriving from Dover had to work over a trailing crossover first. Earlier, in 1898, S.Pearson & Son had laid a siding to the area marked as North Lake for the carriage of ballast required in their Dover Harbour construction work.
(Institute of Civil Engineers Library)

64. The initials IWT referred to the Inland Water Transport Section of the Royal Engineers who were responsible for the construction and operation of the Richborough Military Transportation Depot. Extension of the warehouses of the Robertson Camp is in progress on 19th May 1917.
(Imperial War Museum)

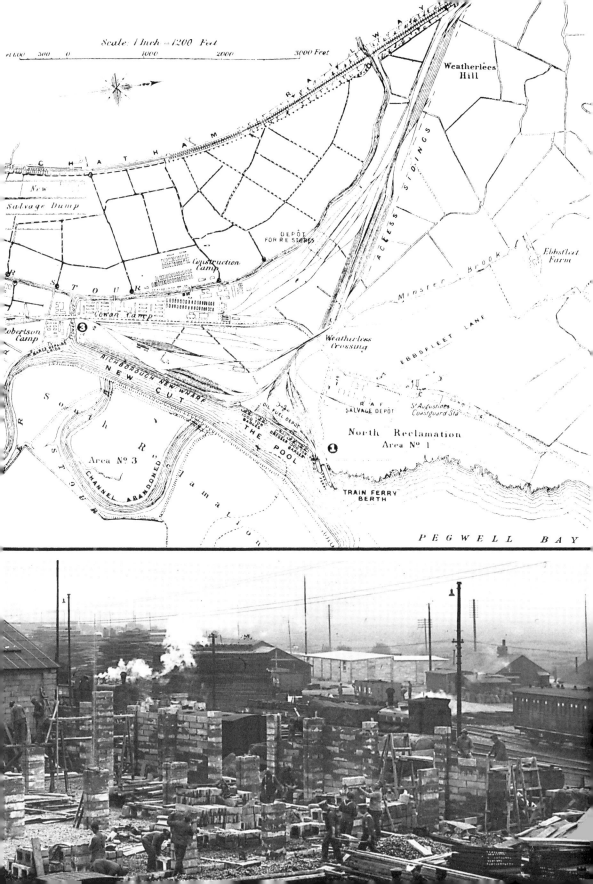

Scale: 1 Inch = 1200 Feet

4'600    300    0    1000    2000    3000 Feet

Weatherlees
Hill

CHATHAM RAILWAY

New
Salvage Dump

DEPÔT
FOR R E STORES

ACCESS SIDINGS

Construction
Camp

STOUR

Cowan Camp

Robertson Camp

Weatherlees
Crossing

Minster Brook

Ebbsfleet
Farm

EBBSFLEET LANE

RICHBOROUGH NEW WHARF

EARLS REPAIRS CRIBS

NEW CUT

South

Area Nº 3

R    CHANNEL ABANDONED    amaltion

STOUR

THE POOL

OIL FUEL DEPOT

R.A.F
SALVAGE DEPÔT

St Augustines
Coastguard Sta.

North Reclamation
Area Nº 1

TRAIN FERRY
BERTH

PEGWELL    BAY

65. The marshalling yard and approach to the train ferry berth was nearly complete when photographed on 23rd December 1917. The extent of the port can be appreciated when this group of sidings is compared with the rest of those shown on the plan.
(Imperial War Museum)

66. The berth was ready for traffic on 10th February 1918 and the train ferries were simply numbered; this is TF3. The unloading and reloading was usually accomplished in under 20 minutes, the 3654 ton ship accommodating 54 wagons. (Miss P. O'Driscoll coll.)

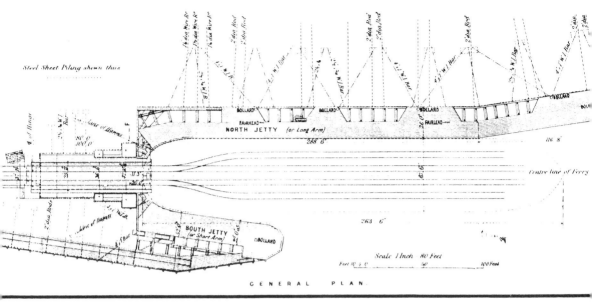

GENERAL PLAN.

The berth was in use until 1921 when the port was sold to the Queenborough Port Co. Ltd. and the ships were sold to operate between Harwich and Zeebrugge, TF1 running until 1957. The position of the ferry deck is shown by the four tracks in the centre of this plan. (Institute of Civil Engineers Library)

67. Two 14" rail mounted guns were shipped to Calais on 26th May 1918, each weighing 296 tons, but the barrels were loaded at Chatham. At its zenith, the port had 31 locomotives, 17 coaches and 519 wagons. (Imperial War Museum)

68. Richborough Castle Halt was opened to the public on 19th June 1933, mainly for the benefit of visitors to the remains of the nearby Roman castle. The halt closed on 11th September 1939, following the advent of WWII. (Lens of Sutton)

The 1939 revision of the 6" to 1 mile map shows much of the WWI track in situ. The area was purchased in 1927 by Pearson & Dorman Long Ltd. who planned to erect a steel works and coking plant that would use fuel from their Kent coalfield. The scheme did not come into being and the port was used only for the export of coal occasionally and the import of some stone and timber. During WWII, the area came under Government control for use by small Naval vessels and the NAAFI, but not as a major port again. In 1943-44, parts of

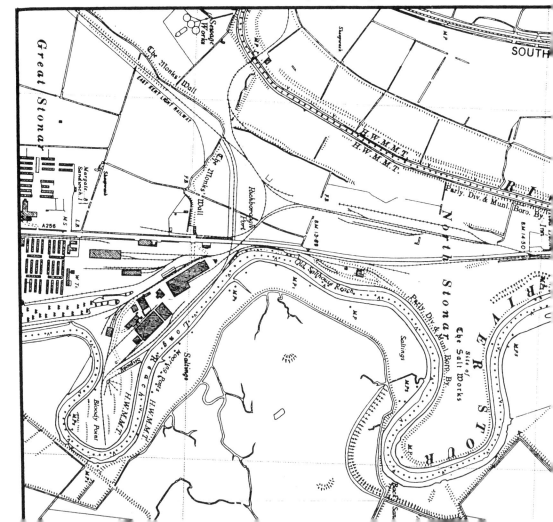

69. The EKR's station looked more like a halt than a terminus. No passenger trains ever arrived here - see our companion album *The East Kent Light Railway*. In the foreground is one of the port lines which crossed the EKR on the level. (A.G.Wells)

Mulberry Harbour were built in the area. After the war, some buildings were again used as colliery workshops, remaining in use until 1953. The EKR and its terminus is shown (upper left) and, in the centre, the Stonar Cut links the two parts of the River Stour. This navigation is fully described in *Kent & East Sussex Waterways* (Middleton Press). In 1962, Richborough Power Station was built to the left of the words MINERAL RAILWAY and the line was thereafter used for the supply of coal to it, primarily from Betteshanger.

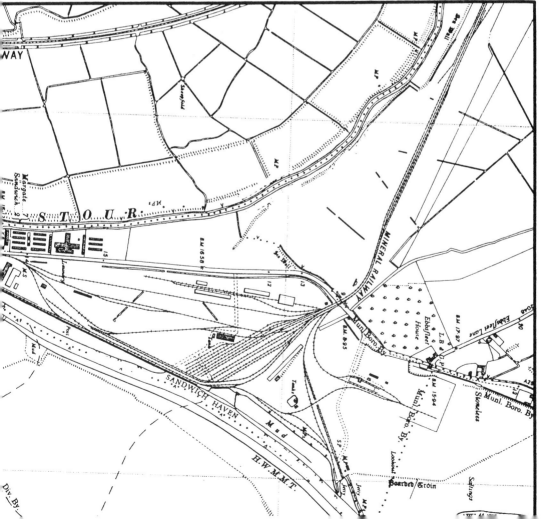

70. After the end of WWII, locomotives used during the liberation of mainland Europe were returned to Britain via the Dover-Dunkirk train ferry. This and the following photographs were taken in 1946 at the Stonar Dump, which was at the south end of the port area. (J.J.Smith)

71. One reporter noted 110 locomotives in store at one period, mainly British built Austerity type 2-8-0s. Many of these were purchased by the LNER. Coal remained in the tenders and not even the chimneys were covered. In some cases the connecting and coupling rods had been removed prior to transhipment. In many instances the locomotives had run low mileages, having been built near the end of the war. (A.G.Wells)

72. Another austerity class for use by the Army was the 0-6-0ST classified J94 by the LNER who bought a batch for shunting work. Many went into industrial use, notably at the colleries, but this example was on general duties at Stonar. (A.G.Wells)

S. E. & C. R. (ISLE THANET)
Available Day of Issue ONLY
Sandwich to
MINSTER
(ISLE OF THANET)
Revised Fare                    Revised Fare
7½d    Third Class    7½d
MINSTER(Thanet) MINSTER(Thanet)

74. On 7th February 1962, a new signal box was opened to serve as a block post and to control access to the sidings to Richborough Power Station. Vandals destroyed the box by fire on 17th August 1988, this photograph dating from May 1981. Betteshanger coal was the primary fuel but oil has been used in recent years, the station being used only infrequently. (D.Cullum)

73. Also at Stonar in 1946 were a number of ex-GWR 0-6-0 Dean goods engines, which had been purchased at the beginning of the war. Several were fitted with Westinghouse air pumps and condensing apparatus, the latter reducing their attraction as a target when moving rail-mounted guns. (A.G.Wells)

75. A rare railtour of the route was the SEG/RCTS "Invicta Invader" which entered the sidings on 5th June 1982. DEMU no. 1012 started from Victoria and ran via London Bridge, Catford Bridge, Orpington, Lea Spur, Gravesend, Grain, Faversham, Richborough, Ashford, Bat & Ball, Nunhead and back to Victoria. (C.Wilson)

76. A southward view in February 1990 shows the commencement of the disused line to the power station and the run-round loop (left). To the right of the redundant cooling tower a wind powered generator was nearing completion. The line crosses the River Stour in the distance, the original bridge consisting of two separate swinging spans. (V.Mitchell)

77. The 10.56 Charing Cross to Ramsgate takes the Minster avoiding line on 24th February 1990, the curve being subject to a 20 mph speed limit. Owing to reduced traffic demand, the connection to Minister was singled. (V.Mitchell)

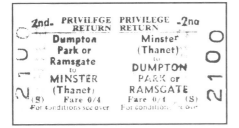

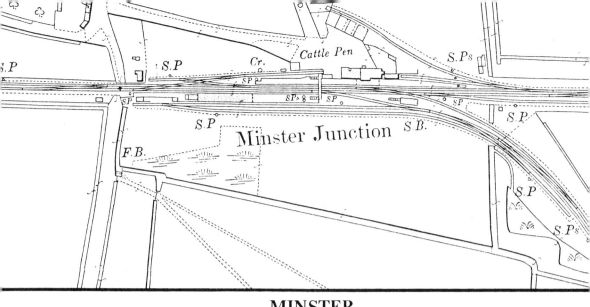

The following labels appear on the map:

S.P · S.P · Cr. · Cattle Pen · S.Ps · S.P · S.P · S.P · S.P · Minster Junction S.B. · S.P · F.B. · S.P · S.Ps

# MINSTER

The branch to Deal was reduced to a single track in 1855 and doubled again in 1865. A bay platform for the Deal branch trains was added in 1872 but it was not until the Dover extension was opened on 15th June 1881 that the triangular junction at Minster came into use. The new loop was closed later, probably as an economy measure during WWI. The 1907 survey shows the position of "A" Box, between the Ashford main line and the bay platform tracks. A new one was opened on 23rd June 1929 when the west side of the triangle was converted to sidings and new connecting lines laid slightly to the east of them. The eastern part of the triangle was reopened at this time.

78. On 7th September 1958, the 12.40pm Ramsgate to Dover service was one of those that ran via Minster. No. 30768 *Sir Balin* ran tender first from Ramsgate, ran round its train and is ready to depart south. (P.Hay)

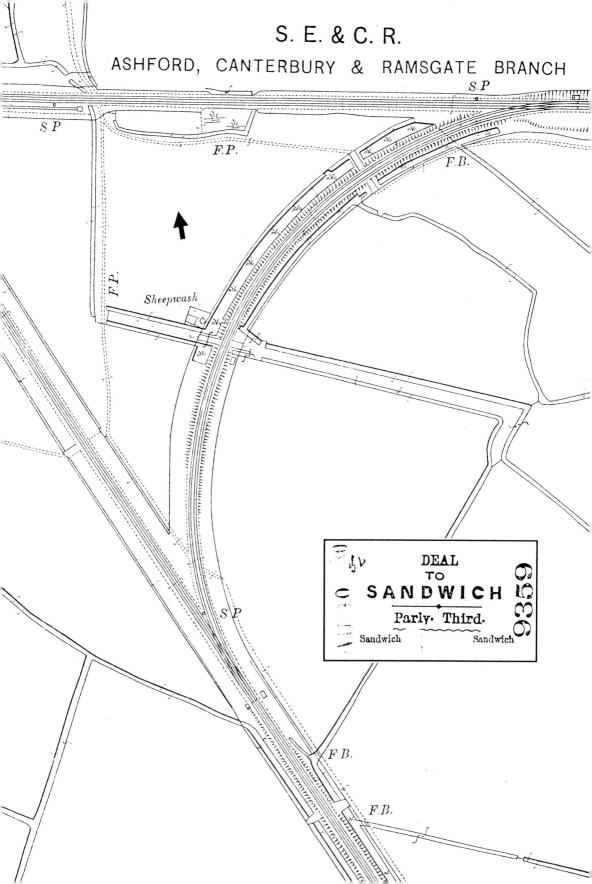

# S. E. & C. R.
## ASHFORD, CANTERBURY & RAMSGATE BRANCH

S.P

S.P

F.P.

F.B.

F.P.

Sheepwash

S.P

F.B.

F.B.

DEAL
TO
**SANDWICH**
Parly. Third.
Sandwich          Sandwich
9359

79. Class U1 2-6-0 no. 31897 is carrying out the same operation on 29th March 1959. This view from the footbridge enables us to see part of the goods yard and 5-ton crane. (A.E.Bennett)

80. An eastward view from the footbridge in 1962 includes the other part of the goods yard, freight facilities being withdrawn on 9th September 1963. Curving away sharply to the right are the sidings that once formed part of the original triangular junction and beyond them is the line to Deal. (Prof. H.P. White)

81. The 1929 Minster "A" signal box was photographed on 4th September 1962. At the time it was built, the nearby village had a population of about 3000. (J.Scrace)

82. Rationalisation was in progress on 14th May 1981, the little used bay platform track having been lifted. The down platform already has a colour light signal at the Ramsgate end. (D.Cullum)

83. Two motor luggage vans were unusual motive power for a Southern Electric Group railtour on 15th March 1986. By then the connection to the Deal line had been singled. (S.C.Nash)

3rd-SINGLE

Minster (Thanet) to

**DUMPTON PARK**

(S)    4½d.H FARE 4½d.H    (S)

For Conditions see over.

0218

0218

84. The historic station was photographed in May 1989 and demolished six months later. The nearby Abbey is one of the oldest religious residences in England. (J.Scrace)

85. The 14.56 from Charing Cross squeals round the curve, prior to reversal to Ramsgate. Since 1981, only a few peak hour trains do this, primarily for the benefit of scholars. (J.Scrace)

# EBBSFLET AND CLIFFSEND

86. The halt was in use between 7th May 1908 and 1st April 1933, serving dwellings adjacent to Pegwell Bay. Transport history was made here in 1968, when the world's first international hoverport was opened. (Lens of Sutton)

87. The Manston-Ramsgate road originally crossed the line on the level. This is now the site of the second road bridge west of Ramsgate. (M.Mirams coll.)

The 1914 revision of the 6" to 1 mile edition shows the location of Ebbsfleet Halt and that the Manston Road still had a level crossing.

# ST. LAWRENCE

88. The station opened in October 1864, the platforms being visible beyond the Newington Road bridge in this westward view. The junction points for the Margate Sands branch are in the foreground. (Lens of Sutton)

89. St. Lawrence was once of greater importance than Ramsgate but early this century it was swallowed up in the latter's suburbs. The site of this country junction is now occupied by the approach to the carriage washers. (M.Mirams coll.)

QUEEN'S AVENUE

F.P.

*Stone*

WHITEHALL

*Whitehall Farm*

*Stone*

*Stones*

S.P.

S.

# S T.

# L A

S.Ps

*Newington*

NEWLANE

S.E. & C.R. (See Back
Available Date of Issue ONLY.

St. LAWRENCE to

**CANTERBURY WEST**

098   098

1/8   Second   1/8

Canterbury W.   Canterbury W.

The 1907 map has the line to Minster on the left, to Margate Sands at the top and those to Ramsgate Town on the right. The station closed on 3rd April 1916.

L O O P   L I N E

*Allotment Gardens*

St. Lawrence
Station   S.B.

F.P.

S.P

S.P

S.P.

*Pavilion*

*Warre Recreation Ground*

F.P.

*Infant School*

*School*

# MARGATE SANDS BRANCH

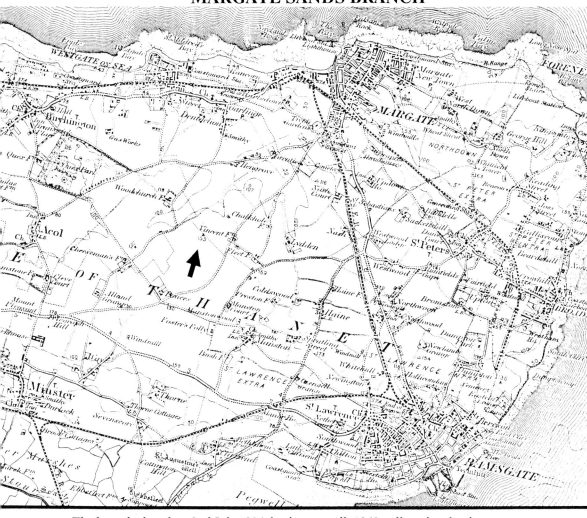

The branch closed on 2nd July 1926, having been Margate's only railway between 1846 and 1863. It is shown near the centre of the 1898 survey which is at 1" to 1 mile, the later LCDR route being on the right. The branch was single until 1863, all trains having to reverse at Ramsgate. The line was doubled during that year and the triangular junction at St. Lawrence was completed.

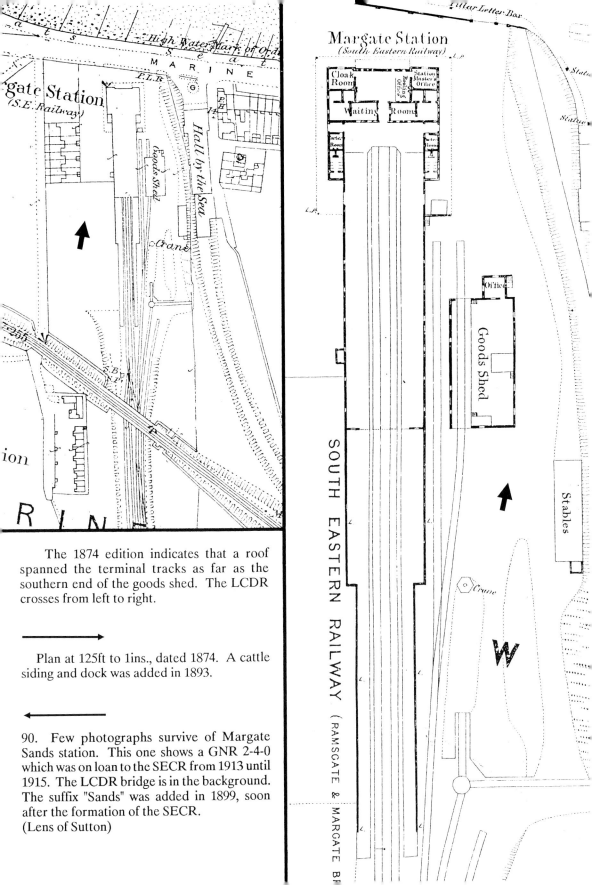

The 1874 edition indicates that a roof spanned the terminal tracks as far as the southern end of the goods shed. The LCDR crosses from left to right.

Plan at 125ft to 1ins., dated 1874. A cattle siding and dock was added in 1893.

90. Few photographs survive of Margate Sands station. This one shows a GNR 2-4-0 which was on loan to the SECR from 1913 until 1915. The LCDR bridge is in the background. The suffix "Sands" was added in 1899, soon after the formation of the SECR.
(Lens of Sutton)

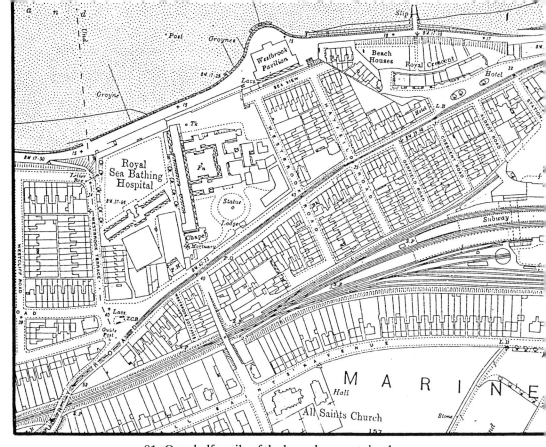

91. Over half a mile of the branch was retained
for use as a loop and headshunt for the goods
yard. This is a northward view from Nash Lane
bridge in August 1950.  (D.Cullum)

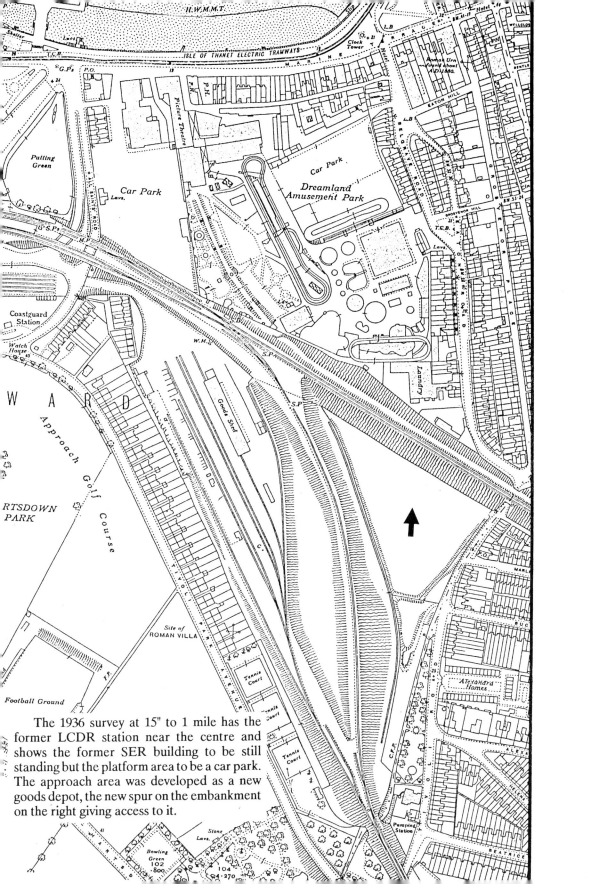

The 1936 survey at 15" to 1 mile has the former LCDR station near the centre and shows the former SER building to be still standing but the platform area to be a car park. The approach area was developed as a new goods depot, the new spur on the embankment on the right giving access to it.

92. The southern limit of the goods line and Nash Lane bridge were photographed on the same day. Further south, the right of way was used for overhead electric cables. (D.Cullum)

The final arrangement of the depot was shown on the control diagram. The yard closed on 1st November 1972, having been used latterly only for coal.

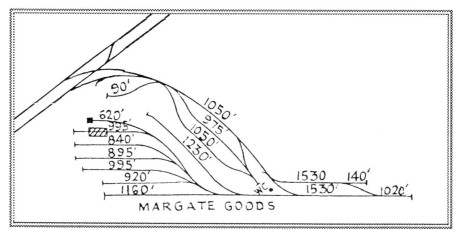

MARGATE GOODS

93. Also recorded on the same day was the site of the SER station, the terminal building being right of centre. (D.Cullum)

94. Another 1956 view shows the front of the terminus and its revised function. The SER certainly had a prime position for tourist traffic. (Prof. H.P. White)

95. The terminus was opened on 13th April 1846, more than six months before that at Margate. There were passenger entrances on the left, as well as those visible on the end of the building. The retaining wall on the right survives. (M.Mirams coll.)

96. The south facade contained Doric columns much loved by the SER in their termini in the 1840s. In the foreground are the tracks of the Isle of Thanet Electric Tramways & Lighting Company. Trams operated between 4th April 1901 and 27th March 1937. (Lens of Sutton)

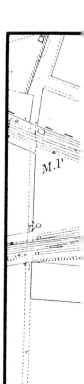

97. SECR no. 191, a class C 0-6-0, awaits departure time and stands at the lengthened platforms. The goods shed and overall roof are also included in this eastward view. (Lens of Suttton)

This 1907 map is almost continuous with that shown for St. Lawrence. Note the tram tracks in the station yard.

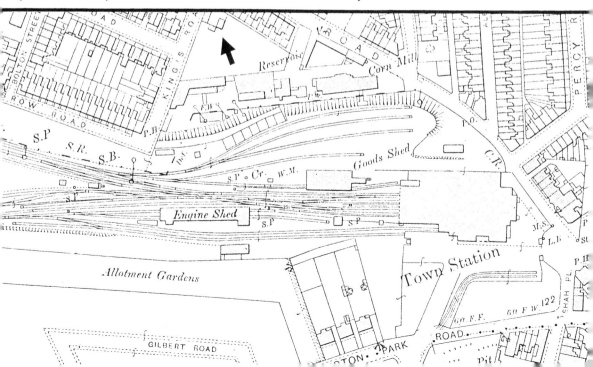

98. The platforms were clearly not long enough for one enthusiastic driver. The notice on the right refers to other drivers - (Lens of Sutton)

*CABMEN, TOWN PORTERS, Etc ARE NOT PERMITTED TO TOUT NOR LOITER UPON THE COMPANYS PREMISES.*

99. Seen in 1913, the overall roof had the inherent disadvantages of the design of trapping locomotive smoke and steam, creating a dingy environment and potentially costly maintenence. (Pamlin Prints)

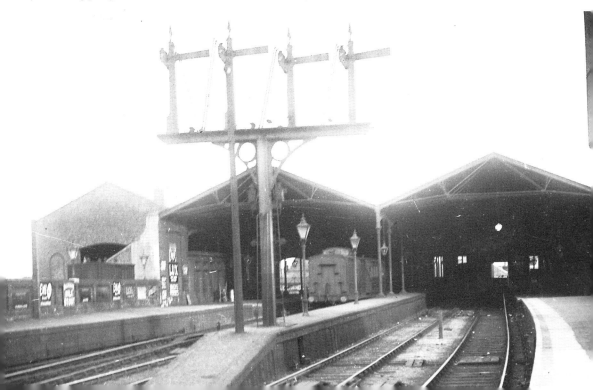

100. After the removal of the roof, the centre platforms were left devoid of covering as they were presumably mainly used by excursion trains. The two-road engine shed and the signal box are visible in the distance. (D.Cullum coll.)

101. F class no. 91 departs with the 10.28am Margate Sands to Dover service on 23rd May 1914 and passes heaps of ash near the depot. No turntable was provided - engines could be turned on the nearby triangular junction. (K.Nunn/LCGB)

# WEST OF RAMSGATE

102. The 1.1pm Birchington to Victoria leaves
Ramsgate on 6th April 1953 behind no. 34067
*Tangmere*. It ran via the Canterbury loop as
flood damage had caused closure of the
Birchington to Herne Bay line. (S.C.Nash)

103. Viewed from Newington Road, three 4VEPs pass the carriage washer, having just arrived as the 09.02 "Thanet Excursion" from Elephant & Castle on 15th August 1985. The rear coaches are on the site of the down platform of St. Lawrence station. (C.Wilson)

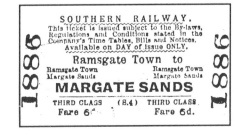

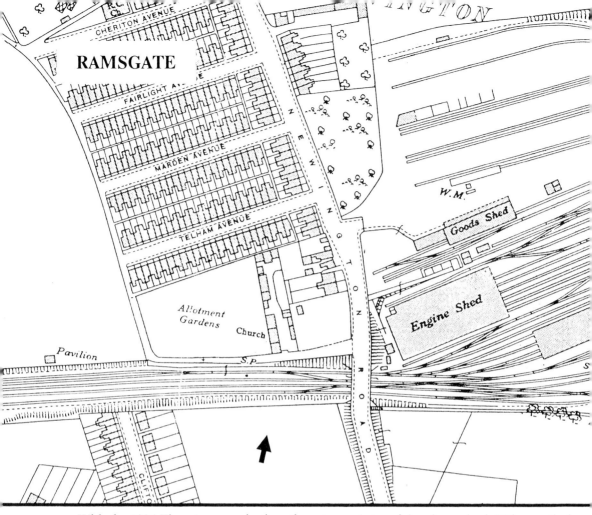

RAMSGATE

With the 1926 Thanet reorganisation, the Town station was abandoned, together with the LCDR Harbour station. A new station and depot were built, mainly within the area of the triangular junction. Its position is shown by two plots of land marked "Dismantled Railway" (right, lower), the western apex being by the widened Newington Road Bridge (left, centre). The map was published in 1938.

104. The new station came into use on 2nd July 1926, when Ramsgate Town was closed. The still clean concrete work was photographed on 3rd March 1928, along with class F no. A241 with its short cab. (H.C.Casserley)

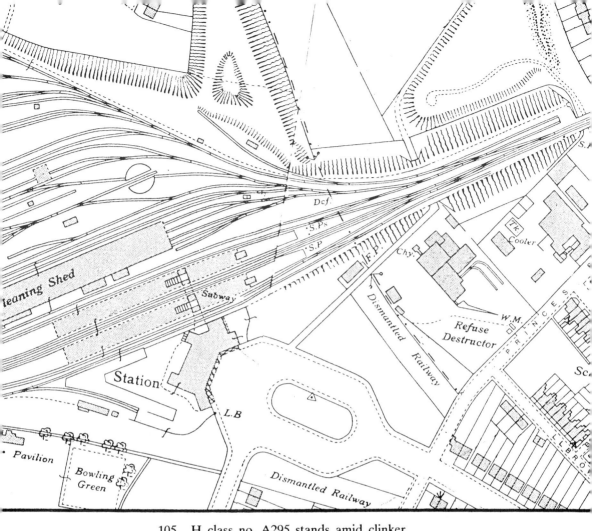

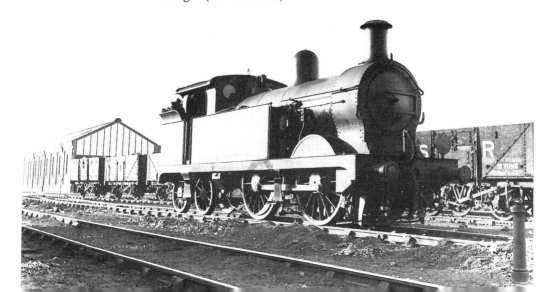

105. H class no. A295 stands amid clinker outside the locomotive shed in 1931. The new well glazed goods shed is in the background. To the right of it, there were seven freight sidings. (J.A.G.Coltas)

106. The mechanical coaling plant is visible in the background of picture no. 104. It saved much labour but broke up the coal and generated much dust, as witnessed on 25th June 1932. (H.C.Casserley)

107. Although apparently unnumbered, ex-SECR O class 0-6-0 no. A98 was in use as a stationary boiler near the carriage cleaning shed on 3rd May 1936. (S.W.Baker)

108. No. 4 lay-by is occupied by Schools class *Downside*, bearing its BR number but SR lettering on its tender. The date is 2nd July 1949, over 18 months after nationalisation. (H.C.Casserley)

109. On the same day, the reverse applied to an ex-LSWR class T9, although the number is prefixed by a small s. On the right is a short dock. It was not used for cattle traffic, this being dealt with between the engine and goods sheds. (H.C.Casserley)

110. Newington Road forms the backdrop as C class no. 31298 plods past with a freight in April 1952, before a rampant lion was applied in place of plain lettering. (P.Hay)

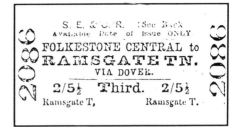

112. On the same day, an H class tank appears to be devoid of signs of ownership, while shunting a Maunsell restaurant car into the cleaning shed. (P.Hay)

111. With lion displayed, class C no. 31004 is in the company of Bulleid Pacifics in April 1952. Behind is the 10,000 gallon water tank and its associated water softener, added in 1933. (P.Hay)

113. The extent of the SR's new station is evident in this 1959 view. Left to right - the engine shed, the carriage cleaning shed, the two island platforms and the church-like booking hall. On the right, insulators await their conductor rails. (Prof. H.P. White)

114. By 28th March 1959, the conductors were in place as no. 34037 *Clovelly* arrives with a train of Bulleid coaches. On the right is C class no. 31245. (R.C.Riley)

115. On the same day, LMR class 4 no. 42090 departs for Ashford while a batch of conductor rails lie waiting to be installed in the cleaning shed. (R.C.Riley)

116. At the time of electrification, other improvements were carried out. The platforms were lengthened (note the "harp" leaning against the nameboard) and the water columns and gaslights (right) were removed. (Lens of Sutton)

117. The 1926 exterior remained little changed in 1959 and indeed is so today. Seldom has a town of 40,000 people seen such a dramtic improvement in facilities and services as Ramsgate did in 1926. (Prof. H.P. White)

118. The electrified sidings were numbered 1 to 29 on the north side of the station, nos. 10 to 13 being in the inspection shed (the former locomotive shed, extended in 1960) and nos. 26 to 28 entering the lifting shed. 4CAP no. 3302 forms the rear part of the 11.44 from Charing Cross on 15th August 1985. (C.Wilson)

119. The 1926 signal box operated mechanical equipment until colour light signals were introduced on 19th July 1959. The box retained its full complement of levers and was photographed in March 1985. (J.Scrace)

120. The location of the signal box is evident in the April 1989 view, as is the flat-roofed train crew accommodation building, added to platforms 3 and 4. An historical vestige is the group of three electrified sidings on the right, which were laid down in 1959 on the route of the old line to Ramsgate Town. (J.Scrace)

## MP Middleton Press

Easebourne Lane, Midhurst. West Sussex. GU29 9AZ
(0730) 813169

## BRANCH LINES

BRANCH LINES TO MIDHURST
BRANCH LINES AROUND MIDHURST
BRANCH LINES TO HORSHAM
BRANCH LINES TO EAST GRINSTEAD
BRANCH LINES TO ALTON
BRANCH LINE TO HAYLING
BRANCH LINE TO SOUTHWOLD
BRANCH LINE TO TENTERDEN
BRANCH LINES TO NEWPORT
BRANCH LINES TO TUNBRIDGE WELLS
BRANCH LINE TO SWANAGE
BRANCH LINES TO LONGMOOR
BRANCH LINE TO LYME REGIS
BRANCH LINE TO FAIRFORD
BRANCH LINE TO ALLHALLOWS
BRANCH LINES AROUND ASCOT
BRANCH LINES AROUND WEYMOUTH
BRANCH LINE TO HAWKHURST
BRANCH LINES AROUND EFFINGHAM JNC

## SOUTH COAST RAILWAYS

CHICHESTER TO PORTSMOUTH
BRIGHTON TO EASTBOURNE
RYDE TO VENTNOR
EASTBOURNE TO HASTINGS
PORTSMOUTH TO SOUTHAMPTON
HASTINGS TO ASHFORD
SOUTHAMPTON TO BOURNEMOUTH
ASHFORD TO DOVER
BOURNEMOUTH TO WEYMOUTH
DOVER TO RAMSGATE

## SOUTHERN MAIN LINES

HAYWARDS HEATH TO SEAFORD
EPSOM TO HORSHAM
CRAWLEY TO LITTLEHAMPTON
THREE BRIDGES TO BRIGHTON
WATERLOO TO WOKING
VICTORIA TO EAST CROYDON
TONBRIDGE TO HASTINGS
EAST CROYDON TO THREE BRIDGES
WOKING TO SOUTHAMLPTON
WATERLOO TO WINDSOR
LONDON BRIDGE TO EAST CROYDON

## COUNTRY RAILWAY ROUTES

BOURNEMOUTH TO EVERCREECH JNC
READING TO GUILDFORD
WOKING TO ALTON
BATH TO EVERCREECH JUNCTION
GUILDFORD TO REDHILL
EAST KENT LIGHT RAILWAY
FAREHAM TO SALISBURY
BURNHAM TO EVERCREECH JUNCTION
REDHILL TO ASHFORD
YEOVIL TO DORCHESTER

## LONDON SUBURBAN RAILWAYS

CHARING CROSS TO DARTFORD

## STEAMING THROUGH

STEAMING THROUGH EAST HANTS
STEAMING THROUGH SURREY
STEAMING THROUGH WEST SUSSEX
STEAMING THROUGH THE ISLE OF WIGHT
STEAMING THROUGH WEST HANTS

## OTHER RAILWAY BOOKS

GARRAWAY FATHER & SON
LONDON CHATHAM & DOVER RAILWAY
INDUSTRIAL RAILWAYS OF THE S. EAST
WEST SUSSEX RAILWAYS IN THE 1980s
SOUTH EASTERN RAILWAYS - due late 1990

## OTHER BOOKS

MIDHURST TOWN THEN & NOW
EAST GRINSTEAD THEN & NOW

WALKS IN THE WESTERN HIGH WEALD
TILLINGBOURNE BUS STORY

MILITARY DEFENCE OF WEST SUSSEX
BATTLE OVER SUSSEX 1940

SURREY WATERWAYS
KENT AND EAST SUSSEX WATERWAYS